Tell Me Why

WHY?

I Can't Eat Peanuts

Katie Marsico

Published in the United States of America by Cherry Lake Publishing
Ann Arbor, Michigan
www.cherrylakepublishing.com

Content Adviser: Lisa K. Militello, PhD, MPH, CPNP, The Ohio State University
Reading Adviser: Marla Conn, ReadAbility, Inc.

Library of Congress Cataloging-in-Publication Data

Marsico, Katie, 1980-
 I can't eat peanuts / by Katie Marsico.
    pages cm. -- (Tell me why)
"Young children are naturally curious about themselves. Tell Me Why I Can't Eat Peanuts offers answers
to their most compelling questions about allergies. Age-appropriate explanations and appealing photos
encourage readers to continue their quest for knowledge. Additional text features and search tools,
including a glossary and an index, help students locate information and learn new words."
—Provided by publisher.
 Audience: Ages 6-10.
 Audience: K to grade 3.
 Includes bibliographical references and index.
 ISBN 978-1-63188-993-6 (hardcover) -- ISBN 978-1-63362-071-1 (pdf) -- ISBN
978-1-63362-032-2 (paperback) -- ISBN (invalid) 978-1-63362-110-7 (ebook)
1. Food allergy in children--Juvenile literature. 2. Peanuts--Juvenile
literature. 3. Food allergy--Juvenile literature. I. Title.

RJ386.5.M363 2015
616.97'5--dc23

                              2014031778

Cherry Lake Publishing would like to acknowledge the work of The Partnership for 21st Century Skills.
Please visit www.p21.org for more information.

Printed in the United States of America
Corporate Graphics

Table of Contents

Careful with Those Cookies! 4

The Power of Peanut 10

Responding to a Reaction 14

Allergy Awareness 18

Think About It 22

Glossary 23

Find Out More 23

Index 24

About the Author 24

Careful with Those Cookies!

Mmm … is someone baking cookies? Pedro's mom says it's snack time! Pedro and his friend Elsa get ready to dig in. But suddenly, Elsa pauses. She asks if the cookies were made with peanuts or peanut products.

Pedro scratches his head. Why is that so important? Doesn't she like peanuts? Elsa tells him she has a peanut **allergy**. She could end up in the hospital if she ate just one peanut.

It can be hard to tell if certain foods have peanuts in them.

Thankfully, Elsa's parents had already shared this information with Pedro's mom. So the cookies have no peanuts in them! As they eat, Pedro's mom explains a little more about allergies to him.

She says that an allergy is the body's **reaction** to a substance. Most people might not be bothered by that substance. For a person with allergies, however, contact with these substances often creates feelings of discomfort and sickness.

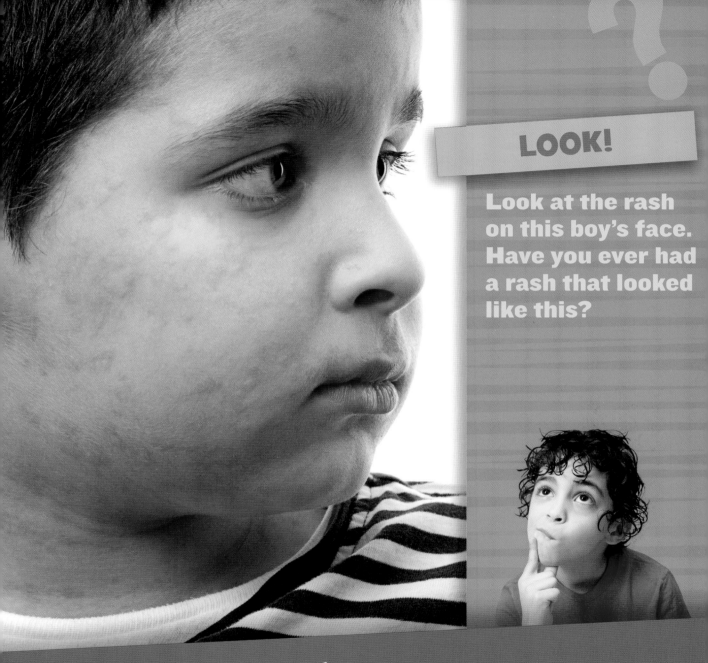

LOOK!

Look at the rash on this boy's face. Have you ever had a rash that looked like this?

An allergy can cause a red bumpy rash.

There are many different kinds of allergies. Some involve foods, chemicals, or medications. Others are caused by dust, dandruff, pollen, or insect bites.

Skin rashes, sneezing, and itching are signs of an allergic reaction. So are difficulty breathing, stomach problems, and changes in **blood pressure**. A very serious allergic reaction can cause a condition called anaphylactic shock. People who get this need immediate medical attention or they could die.

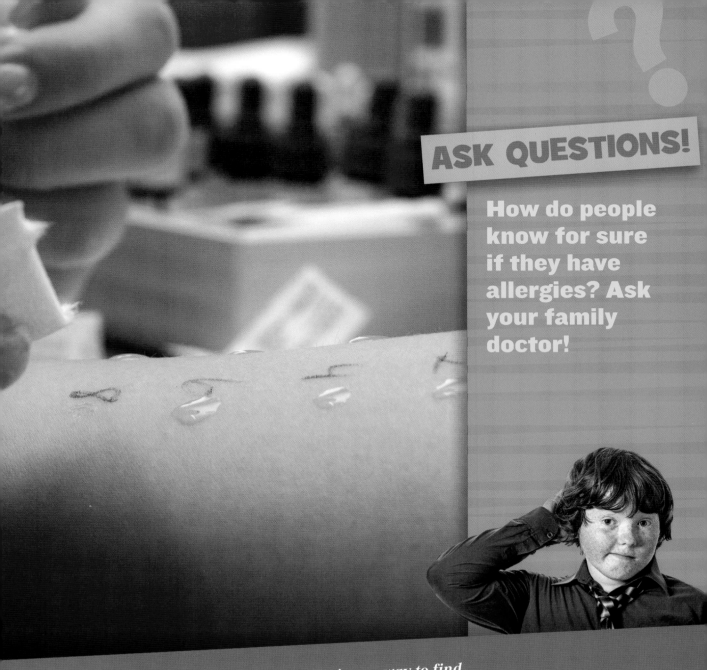

ASK QUESTIONS!

How do people know for sure if they have allergies? Ask your family doctor!

An allergy test done in a doctor's office is one way to find out if someone is allergic to peanuts or other foods.

The Power of a Peanut

Pedro still feels puzzled. How does something as tiny as a peanut have the power to make his friend so sick? His mom replies that it's because of how Elsa's **immune system** reacts to the peanut.

Usually, this body system battles illness and disease. But sometimes it gets confused and tries to fight off substances that don't normally cause illness. In Elsa's case, her immune system overreacts to the **proteins** found in peanuts.

Not all people can eat peanuts.

When Elsa eats peanuts or peanut products, her body launches an attack. It does this by releasing **histamines** into her bloodstream. These chemicals create the unpleasant **symptoms** that someone with an allergy experiences.

Medicines often provide relief from mild allergic reactions. People with severe allergies often require stronger treatment. Many also need to take extra steps to prevent allergic reactions from occurring in the first place.

Are you able to guess what other foods trigger allergic reactions? Eggs are one. Try to name a few more!

Some people are allergic to fish, bread, or milk.

Responding to a Reaction

Pedro thinks Elsa is one brave girl! What happens if she accidentally eats peanuts or a peanut product? What if she can't get to a hospital right away?

Elsa says that's why she always carries **epinephrine** with her. This medicine is usually given as a shot into the side of a person's thigh. Then it enters the bloodstream and begins fighting the effects of a serious allergic reaction.

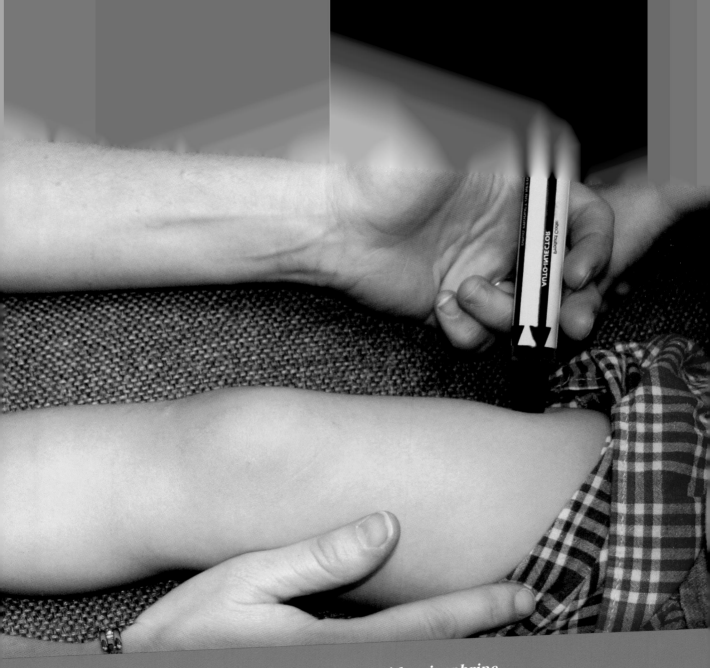

This tube has a needle inside it that is filled with epinephrine.

Epinephrine forces people's **blood vessels** to tighten. In turn, their blood pressure drops, and their chest muscles relax. This makes it easier to breathe. Epinephrine also helps bring down swelling and soothes itchiness. Most of the time, a shot of epinephrine starts working in just a few minutes.

It's always a good idea to visit a doctor following a serious allergic reaction.

Allergy Awareness

Thank goodness Elsa won't need a shot! Normally, she doesn't use epinephrine because she limits her contact with peanuts.

One way she does this is by reading food labels. Elsa and her family make people aware of her allergy, too. When she eats out, cafeteria and restaurant workers are often able to provide peanut-free food choices.

Many school cafeterias provide peanut-free food.

The way Elsa's snacks and meals are prepared is also important. Neither the food nor the silverware can be near a surface that has touched peanuts.

Elsa admits that living with a peanut allergy is sometimes challenging. But she's grateful to Pedro and his mom for being helpful. Dealing with a peanut allergy is easier when others are aware of it and understand. Of course, a batch of tasty, peanut-free cookies helps, too!

Peanut-free cookies are a safe choice for a snack, if they are safely prepared.

Think About It

Why do some people have food allergies while others don't? Scientists know that a person is more likely to suffer from food allergies if his or her parents do. Why do you think this is?

Unlike tree nuts such as almonds and walnuts, peanuts are legumes. Yet people who are allergic to peanuts are often allergic to tree nuts, too. Why do you think this is the case?

People with peanut allergies have to worry about far more than peanut butter. Think about what other foods are made with peanuts or peanut products.

Glossary

allergy (AH-luhr-jee) a physical reaction that causes someone to get sick after eating, touching, or breathing something that is harmless to most people

blood pressure (BLUHD PREH-shuhr) the force with which blood flows through a person's body

blood vessels (BLUHD VEH-suhlz) tubes that carry blood throughout the body

epinephrine (eh-puh-NEH-fruhn) a medication used to treat severe allergic reactions

histamines (HIS-tuh-meenz) chemicals produced by the immune system that create the symptoms of an allergic reaction

immune system (ih-MYOON SIS-tuhm) the network of cells, tissues, and organs that work together to protect the body

proteins (PROH-teenz) naturally produced substances that are found in foods and that sometimes trigger allergic reactions

reaction (ree-AK-shuhn) a response

symptoms (SIMP-tuhmz) physical signs that often hint at a health problem

Find Out More

Books:

Jacobs, Jessica, and Jacquelyn Roslyn (illustrator). *The Peanut Pickle: A Story About Peanut Allergy.* New York: Sky Pony Press, 2012.

McClure, Wendy, and Tammie Lyon (illustrator). *The Princess and the Peanut Allergy.* New York: AV2 by Weigl, 2013.

Nelson, Maria. *I'm Allergic to Peanuts.* New York: Gareth Stevens Publishing, 2014.

Web Sites:

AllergyHome.org—Free Downloadable Food Allergy Posters
http://www.allergyhome.org/teach/
Download, print, and hang posters to help spread awareness about food allergies in your community!

KidsHealth—Nut and Peanut Allergy
http://kidshealth.org/kid/stay_healthy/food/nut_allergy.html
Learn more about what a peanut allergy involves, as well as how this health condition is treated.

Index

allergy, 4, 6-8, 13
allergy test, 9
anaphylactic shock, 8

cafeteria, 18-19
cause, 10, 12, 22

epinephrine, 14-16

food preparation, 4-6, 20-22

histamines, 12

immune system, 10

prevention, 12, 18-20

rash, 7-8
reaction, 4, 6-8, 16
treatment, 12, 14-17

tree nuts, 22

About the Author

Katie Marsico is the author of more than 150 children's books. She lives in a suburb of Chicago, Illinois, with her husband and children.